Travels w… Magell…

The Story of Ferdinand Magellan

Alison Hawes

Contents

OXFORD
UNIVERSITY PRESS

OXFORD
UNIVERSITY PRESS

Great Clarendon Street, Oxford OX2 6DP

Oxford University Press is a department of the University of Oxford. It furthers the University's objective of excellence in research, scholarship, and education by publishing worldwide in

Oxford New York

Auckland Cape Town Dar es Salaam Hong Kong Karachi Kuala Lumpur Madrid Melbourne Mexico City Nairobi New Delhi Shanghai Taipei Toronto

With offices in
Argentina Austria Brazil Chile Czech Republic France Greece Guatemala Hungary Italy Japan Poland Portugal Singapore South Korea Switzerland Thailand Turkey Ukraine Vietnam

Oxford is a registered trade mark of Oxford University Press in the UK and in certain other countries

First published 2003

British Library Cataloguing in Publication Data

Data available

ISBN: 978-0-19-919532-9

20 19 18 17 16 15 14 13 12 11

True Stories Pack 1 (one of each title) ISBN 978-0-19-919537-4
True Stories Pack 1 Class Pack (six of each title) ISBN 978-0-19-919536-7

Acknowledgements

The publisher would like to thank the following for permission to reproduce photographs:

Front cover background artwork: Tony Chance
Inset photo: Scala
Back cover: Hulton Archive.

Illustrations are by Tony Chance
Map is by Richard Morris

Printed in China by Imago

Introduction

In 1519 Ferdinand Magellan sailed from Spain to find a new **route** to the **Spice Islands**.

One of the men who sailed with Magellan wrote a book about their **voyage**.

This book tells his personal story of the long and dangerous journey.

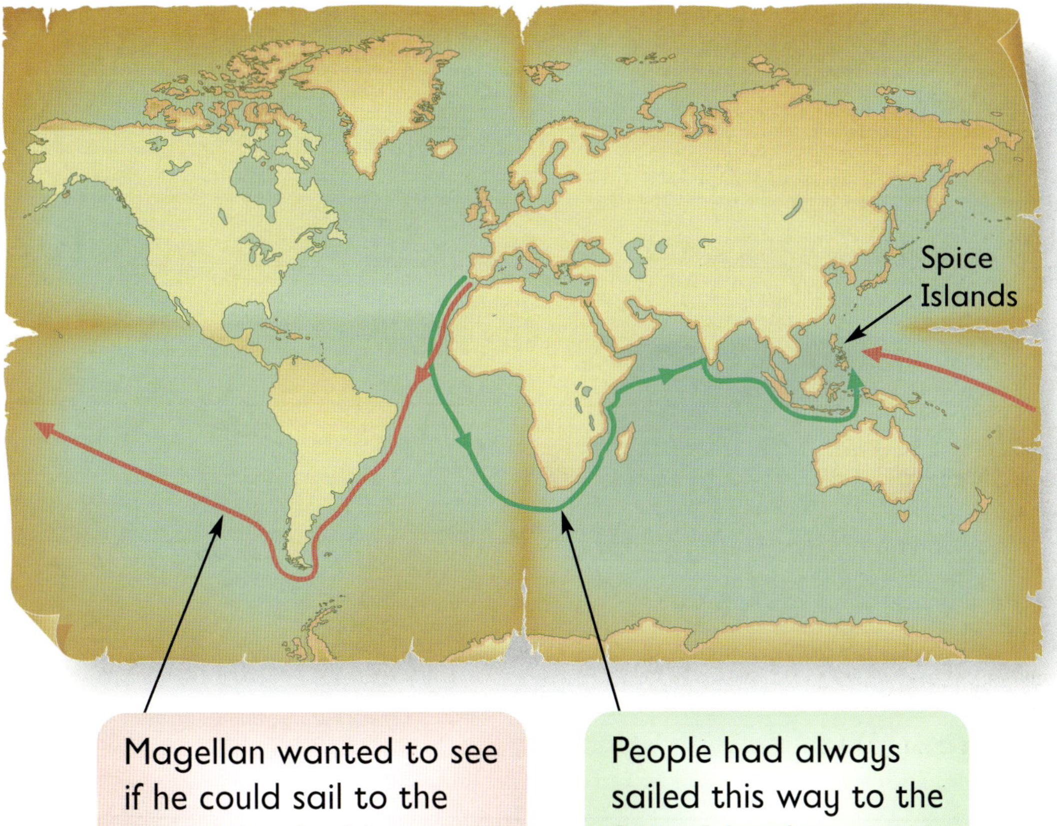

Chapter 1

Spain

I met a man called Magellan. He was looking for adventure. He was going to sail to the Spice Islands.

I wasn't a sailor, but I was looking for adventure too. He let me go with him.

I put all our adventures down in a book.

September 1519

When we left, Magellan said, "We are going to sail where no one has sailed before!"

But some of the sailors were frightened they would get lost. They were afraid a giant sea monster would eat them up.

"We want to go the way we know," the sailors said.

But Magellan said "No!"

So the sailors did as Magellan said.

As we sailed we saw new animals we had not seen before. We saw whales and seals and squid. We saw black and white birds that could not fly. We saw fish that could fly!

Chapter 2
Brazil

December 1519

We sailed to new lands.

We met new people and made friends with them. We gave them mirrors and cloth. They gave us new foods we had not seen before.

We set sail again.

It became colder and colder. Soon all of our five ships were thick with ice.

"It is too cold to sail," said Magellan. "We must stop here for a bit."

Some of the men didn't want to stop on land. They were frightened and wanted to go home.

But Magellan said "No!"

Some of the men wanted to kill him then. Magellan found out and stopped them.

Chapter 3
Patagonia

March 1520

It was winter so we stayed on land. We made huts to live in. We cleaned and mended our ships.

We met some people and made friends with them. They were very tall people. They helped us to look for food.

We caught crabs and fish. We hunted for birds and animals. We packed some of the food to take with us.

May 1520

At last we were ready to go. But when we set off, we sailed into a big storm. One of the ships crashed into some rocks.

Just in time, the men jumped into the water.

The ship broke up, but the men made it to land. Magellan picked them up in his ship.

Chapter 4
Pacific Ocean

November 1520

Some months later we sailed into more bad storms.

Suddenly the men on one ship set sail for home.
"They have taken lots of our food!" we said.
Magellan couldn't stop them.
We had just three ships left now.

At last the storms stopped. The sun came out and it was very hot.

"We have very little food left," we said.

Magellan said, "When we see land, we will stop and get food and water."

But we sailed and sailed and we saw no land.

Our food began to rot in the hot sun. Soon the food was so rotten we couldn't eat it. All we had to eat were rats and **sawdust**!

Our water went bad and turned yellow. It was so bad we had to hold our noses to drink it.

Lots of people died.

Chapter 5

Guam

March 1521

Magellan said, "We must get to land soon or we will all die!"

Then, just in time, we saw an island. There was lots of food and water on the island. But the island people were not friendly. They took things from our ships and would not let us have food and water.

"But we must have food or we will all die!" said Magellan.

So in the end we had to fight the island people.

We took lots of their food and water. Then we sailed away to look for another island.

Chapter 6

Philippine Islands

March 1521

Soon we came to lots of islands. On one island we made friends with the people.

We had a good rest and we soon became well. The island people gave us food. It tasted spicy.

"We must be getting closer to the Spice Islands!" said Magellan.

27th April, 1521

Then one day our new friends were attacked by people from another island.

We tried to help our friends but there were too many people for us to fight.

Magellan yelled to us, "Run back to the ships!"

We ran, but on the way Magellan was killed.

Sadly we sailed away without Magellan.

One of our ships began to sink. It was full of big cracks. The wood had been eaten by worms. It could not be mended so we set fire to it.

For many months we lived as pirates.
We robbed people and took their gold.

We all wanted to go home.
“We can’t give up,’” said one of the men.
“We must sail on to the Spice islands.”

Chapter 7

Spice Islands

November 1521

Finally, after many months, we arrived at the Spice Islands.

We filled our ships with spices and set sail for home.

One ship began to crack. It had to sail back to the Spice Islands to be mended.

So we went home in the one ship we had left.

September 1522

Lots of people died on the way home. Just 19 of us got back.

We had found a new way to the Spice Islands, and we had sailed around the world. We had been away for three years.

We were happy to be home.

Antonio Pigafetta

Glossary

Pacific Ocean the name Magellan gave to the largest ocean in the world

Patagonia land near the tip of South America

route a way to get from one place to another

sawdust the powder left from sawing wood

spice part of a plant that is dried and used to flavour food

Spice Islands a group of islands in the Pacific Ocean where many spices are grown

voyage a long journey

Index